No One Ever Taught Me How to Learn

How to Unlock Your Learning Potential and Become Unstoppable

By I. C. Robledo

www.Amazon.com/author/icrobledo

No One Ever Taught Me How to Learn: How to Unlock Your Learning Potential and Become Unstoppable

Copyright © 2015 by Issac Robledo.

Disclaimer

TABLE OF CONTENTS

INTRODUCTION

Why does Learning Matter?

I think we all have a pretty good idea about why learning matters, but I believe it's important to review why it is especially relevant today. We live in a time when there are many world issues that are constantly evolving, and that demand for educated and learned individuals to evaluate complex scenarios. Some of these issues are: poverty, hunger, climate change, limited energy, pollution, the threat of nuclear warfare, and a lack of education. To tackle such problems, among many others, will require people who take learning seriously, and don't jump to conclusions in their search for answers. Of course, no one book or learning approach can tackle all such problems. But I think we can agree that people who work to improve their learning ability will be more likely to put a dent in finding solutions.

As another matter, learning will be an important part of the modern worker's life. According to the Bureau of Labor Statistics (BLS), baby boomers held an average of eleven jobs from the ages 18 to 46. It seems likely that most workers going into the future will hold at least that many in their lifetimes. With each new job, new skills may need to be learned. Also, many people who attend college will find a job or career that is outside of their major area of study. According to a CareerBuilder survey of 2,134 workers, 47% of college educated workers took a first job that was unrelated to their major, and 32% of college educated workers never found a job related to their major. According to such findings, it is likely new workers will have plenty to learn upon entry into their first job as it may be unrelated to the field they studied in college. Jobs are also demanding more and more from the employees that they do have, due to economic concerns and the drive to increase profits. People with solid learning skills will likely find themselves much better able to learn the new skills needed, and to compete when looking for employment.

The prior points don't even consider that knowledge itself is growing and changing. Facts that were once well accepted no longer are. The usual example is that we once believed the world was flat. Of course, we don't need to go back that far to find an example. Nutritional advice has shifted greatly over the past hundred years. As Michael Pollan reviews, in "In Defense of Food", in the 1950s margarine was seen as a healthy alternative to butter since it didn't have saturated fat, then years later it was found that the trans-fats in margarine were even worse than the saturated fats they replaced. Of course by this point people no longer thought margarine was so healthy. The knowledge and information available to the public had completely changed. As another example, it wasn't so long ago (from 2006 and earlier) that Pluto was taught in schools as being a planet. It was viewed as a planet for 76 years. Now, it is believed to be one of many large icy bodies in the outer solar system, and is no longer defined as a planet by scientists.

With the internet and better technological equipment, knowledge is growing and growing. What was seen as true even ten years ago or less may now be viewed as a misconception or as false. With the vast spread of information also comes a spread of misinformation. Not everything we learn today will be seen as correct in the future, and so it's important that we take some time to think about what we are learning, and how we learn it.

In essence, there are many reasons why learning is more important now than ever before. For example, we face an ever growing list of world problems to deal with, people are changing jobs more which demand learning new skills, and the information available to us is expanding faster and faster. We must prepare ourselves for a rapidly changing and evolving world. Part of this preparation will be in training ourselves to learn with sound techniques, rather than learning based on myths or with little direction.

Introducing Learning as a Powerful Skill

You may be thinking that every field or skill requires a different way to learn it. To learn piano may be different from mathematics, which may be different from painting. This can be true. For that reason it is always helpful to have an instructor or a tutor, but there are also some solid principles of learning that should generally hold true regardless of the specific content that you want to learn. Those learning principles can be learned and applied to different fields and skills.

The thing to understand is that learning is a skill like any other. Of course, it can take some instruction and practice to become a good learner. Most importantly, you should realize that even if you've been labeled a slow learner, or a bad learner, there are ways to improve your learning. This is because learning itself is a skill that can be improved upon. It's not a static part of you that can never be changed.

It's a shame that as a society we often focus strictly on the content that is to be learned, rather than the process of learning itself. We often are expected to learn something new, and to learn it fast and accurately. But what if you've developed bad learning habits? And what if you are overconfident that your particular learning techniques are effective, but they're in fact counterproductive. You may be surprised to find that such mistakes are quite common. The particular techniques which are more effective or less so will be discussed later in this book to help you on the path to learning effectively and ridding yourself of bad habits.

What if there was one skill you could acquire that would help you in all areas of your life? Wouldn't you want to take the time to learn that one skill? Perhaps you want to improve your performance in school, or understand computer programs better, or play an instrument better. Of course, if that were the case you could read books or find an instructor in those areas, and that would make perfect sense. But another way to tackle the problem is to realize that you will always be faced with new things to learn. Learning is something that will be important for you throughout your life, and it would make great sense to improve your ability to learn. If you work on that one skill, you can improve in multiple areas more efficiently.

As you've hopefully started to notice, learning can be quite a powerful skill to have. If you advance in your ability to learn, you may be more competitive in your work, resulting in a more secure employment for yourself. You may find that you are smarter than you thought. Perhaps you were just using bad or ineffective techniques for learning all through your life, and when you start using effective ways of learning your performance will improve across the board. By putting in the effort to improve your skill at learning, you will have more power to quickly and effectively understand material and to acquire new and important skills.

Let's discuss what happens if you aren't a good learner in society. People with a poor ability to learn will tend to reach their limits fairly early on. They will find themselves in a job position where they're unable to advance any further. Their superiors, noticing that the worker is not particularly fast or capable in their learning, will be reluctant to promote him. Those with bad learning skills will tend to perform worse in school, on the job, and in other areas of life as well. It's a sad predicament, but one that can be avoided for most people if they were to focus on viewing learning as a skill that can be improved. The worst mistake that can be made is to assume that your ability to learn is fixed and that you have no control over it. This could result in stagnation and even poorer performance.

Why hasn't Anyone Taught me to Learn Properly?

The science of learning has recently made great advancements. Throughout much of history we simply did not have good information on how we learn, effective ways to learn, or how to improve our learning. The good news is that we now have solid scientific findings that can show us how to be better learners and get the results we want in our lives. Of course, scientists are always conducting new studies and advancing their understanding of how we learn, but we currently have a good foundation from which we can begin improving our own learning.

You probably weren't taught about learning because there was not solid science behind what may work or not work when it came to learning. When teachers don't know something, they would likely prefer to ignore the topic. Unfortunately, many students will go through the school system with inadequate learning skills. Not having been taught to learn, they may continue along that path for most or all of their lives, achieving worse results than they could have with proper instruction.

Reasons for Learning

There are many different reasons to learn. Of course, we will all have different and personal ones. The following are some of the main reasons for learning, and for which this book could be helpful.

Reliable Employment. Improving employability is something many people are interested in. Unfortunately, we often don't consider how important learning is as a skill until we find ourselves unemployed. At that point, it can be overwhelming to have to deal with finding a job, making money, and acquiring new competitive skills all at the same time. With all of those pressures, a person is likely to seek out any job they can find in their desperation. When you focus on improving your ability to learn, and on learning new things on a regular basis, you'll find that you've gradually acquired new skills and abilities, and be more confident and able to learn new things that come your way. You will be more competitive, less likely to be let go by your employer, and more likely to find the job you want.

In the times we live, employers and employees feel less loyalty to each other than they may have in the early to mid-1900s. The reality is that employers can fire employees for almost any reason, and it can happen at any time. The worker may not have even done anything wrong. Perhaps there just isn't the money in the budget, or the performed job has been declared unnecessary for the future goals of the company. It's important for workers in the modern age to be prepared and to constantly learn new skills and abilities. Take advantage of the work climate and learn new things on the job when possible. If you have spare time or periods of low activity while at work, don't waste it. Use that time to expand your understanding of your work. You may read a book on an important issue, try out a new program or procedure, or volunteer to help someone else who performs different tasks than you. A worker who does these things will be the kind of worker who is much less likely to be fired, and even if she were, she would find a new job fairly easily. The worker who becomes too comfortable and never bothers to learn anything new will be one of the first to go when the company decides it needs to conduct layoffs.

School and University. Perhaps you are taking classes at school or at a university. With this kind of learning, you'll have a specific topic that is important to you. Perhaps you wish to get a job in that field, or you may wish to improve your skills. With classroom learning, you will follow the guidance of your instructor. He will point out the material that you need to learn, and expect you to study it and memorize it. This is a very common kind of learning, and despite the structured curriculum, students should remember that they could still benefit from using sound study and learning techniques. Many students who do poorly in school will do so because they were unaware of the ineffective study techniques that they used.

Independent Learning. Another form of learning is independent learning, which anyone can do. A student, teacher, or adult could engage in independent learning. All that is required is the desire to learn something new, and the willingness to seek out materials or resources to learn about the topic. With this kind of learning, there isn't necessarily one instructor who can guide your path. It may not be clear what you need to begin learning first, what the best structure is to learning, or even what materials may be best to pursue your goals. Because of these reasons, usually you will need to have a strong drive to pursue independent learning. The learner is likely to be met with some frustration on their path to discovering how to properly learn for themselves. Nonetheless, it can be a great experience to try learning for yourself. It will be very helpful for the independent learner to have a solid foundation in effective learning approaches and techniques.

Skills. Acquiring new skills is another form of learning. This one can overlap with other types of learning. In school we usually learn through books. In that stage we are reading and memorizing definitions of concepts, and then understanding how key concepts relate to each other. Learning skills, on the other hand, is based more on practice and repetition. It's often more critical to have an instructor or tutor of some kind to ensure that the proper techniques are being used. For example, when learning piano you have to learn not just which keys to hit as you read the sheet music, but you have to know the proper posture, hand positioning, and technique for moving your hands as you play the notes. This is to reduce the chance of injury and to make it easier to play fluidly and naturally as you learn more and more complex pieces. As we see, in some cases it is important to have the right guidance to make sure that we make progress in our learning goals.

Mastery. Perhaps you want to be a master of your domain. You've defined the topic that interests you, and you've decided that you want to be the best in that field. That is admirable, and certainly it makes sense that if you know what you want to pursue, that you put everything you have into improving in that one domain. Someone who wants to be the best will often need to have great motivation, a complete focus on their goal, and proper instruction. Sometimes the proper instruction isn't available in the beginning, and it will be necessary to teach yourself or to learn from books. Eventually, with the right talent and intense motivation you may attract a good mentor or find that you have been able to improve your abilities on your own. There are many paths that lead to mastery, but consistent effort is essential.

Strengthening weaknesses. Another reason to learn would be to improve weaknesses. It can be frustrating to hear over and over that you are not good at a particular topic or at a certain skill. Hearing it time and again from different people can become frustrating, and you may accept the criticism as truth as time passes. It can be a mistake to ignore or neglect weaknesses – they will not go away on their own. If you find that you have a weakness that is important to you personally, or to your work, it can make sense to work specifically on building up that weakness to the level you'd like. Knowing how to learn properly will be important for making improvements on your weak areas.

The common feature of all of these examples is that improving your skill at learning will make all of these kinds of learning go by more easily, fluidly, and you can even have some fun with it. It's much better to have an approach or a system to learning, than it is to just see it as something that you have no control over. When you take control of your learning, you have a much better chance to influence the outcome in your favor. In this book I hope to show you how you can use this powerful skill to your advantage. No matter if you are learning in school, at home, at work, or in other areas of your life and for whatever purpose, the aim of this book is to help you improve your understanding of the learning process so you can begin achieving better results.

BEFORE YOU CONTINUE . . .

As a thank you for reading, I want you to have a free guide called:

Step Up Your Learning: Free Tools to Learn Almost Anything

Have you ever wondered what the best sites and resources for learning are? It takes time and effort to figure out which sites are worth it and which are not. I hope to save you some of that time so you can spend more of it learning instead of searching the Internet.

In the past ten years or so, there has been a free learning revolution happening. More and more resources for learning are becoming available to the public at no cost. With so many new ones coming out, it's easy to miss out on some of the great learning opportunities available. Fortunately for you, this guide is short at around 4,000 words, and tells you exactly what you need to know.

The guide stems from my own experiences of using a variety of learning sites and resources. In it, you will discover the best places to go for learning at no cost. Also, I'll explain which resources are best for you, depending on your learning goals.

You can download this free guide as a PDF by typing this website into your browser:

http://bit.ly/Robledo

Now, let's get back on topic.

MYTHS ABOUT LEARNING

There are quite a few myths or misconceptions when it comes to learning. It's easy to fall into the trap of believing these myths unless you are specifically taught that they are faulty. In this section I will go through some of the most common and harmful misconceptions that some people believe.

I believe it's important to start with the misconceptions because there are many of them, and I want us all to be on the same page and on the same level of understanding. It's best if we get the facts straight before we move forward on trying to advance our own learning.

Myth #1: There isn't Much we Can do to Improve our Abilities

Dr. Carol Dweck has done some research regarding people's beliefs about their own abilities. Her findings were very interesting and somewhat surprising. She tested how people's beliefs influenced their abilities. Some people believe that their abilities are fixed, and there isn't much they can do to improve. *They're either good at something or bad at it, and there is no changing it.* Other people tend to believe that if they work hard at something, they can improve their abilities. *They can get better through hard work.* In her research, she found that people who thought their abilities were fixed were more likely to give up when they faced difficult problems. People who thought they could improve would not give up so easily, and would persist in working on them.

Why are her findings important? Persisting in working on tough problems is a big part of learning. Learning is not a simple thing that happens automatically and without effort. It takes some time, effort, and persistence. The first big step to learning will be to realize that your learning goal may be a challenge, it may be quite difficult, but with steady progress you can always improve.

Those who do not believe they have a good chance to do well at a task will often give up early and eliminate the possibility that they may learn something new and useful.

Myth #2: You are Good at Assessing Your own Ability Levels

We all naturally seem to believe that we can judge whether we are good at something or not. Maybe some of us can, but for the most part, as Dunning and Kruger have indicated through their research, there is reason for us to be suspicious of how we judge our own ability levels.

Essentially, the **Dunning-Kruger effect** shows that people who are more skilled will tend to underestimate their own abilities, whereas people who are less skilled will tend to overestimate their abilities. In other words, someone who performs quite well at a task is likely to be less confident, and someone who performs poorly at the same task is likely to be overconfident in their abilities.

Why would this happen? It seems that the lower ability people are not informed enough to realize how little they truly know. They assume that they perform pretty well because they simply don't know any better. They haven't received enough evidence yet to show them that they actually are not performing well at all.

The higher ability people, on the other hand, will tend to perform fairly well without putting too much effort into the given task. Perhaps they've gradually acquired the experience through the years or they have a high natural ability. In any case, because they perform well fairly easily, they assume the task will be easy for others as well, when in reality it is not. Therefore, they underestimate their own ability.

The main point is that we shouldn't trust our perceptions of our own abilities completely. We should seek feedback from professionals if we wish to get a good idea of how good we are in a given skill or topic. In any case, an important point we should remember is that no matter our skill level, there is always room for improvement.

Myth #3: Easy Learning Means Good Learning

This is a big myth. Most people just seem to assume that if they understand something quite easily, with little effort on their part, that it means the topic is easy, and it means they understand the topic quite well. Actually, this situation will often lead to easy forgetting. Since the material wasn't especially challenging and didn't require much effort or work to figure out, the brain didn't have a chance to fully understand and connect the material to other known concepts. As a result, the learning is of poor quality, and the material is soon forgotten. Even if it isn't forgotten, it's unlikely to be fully understood or learned well enough to apply it in any meaningful way.

In contrast to the above, the more you have to work to learn something, the more likely it is that the material will be well learned and understood. If you choose to add challenges that make learning more difficult, this will actually improve your learning experience. At first, the added challenge may not seem beneficial. Your performance may suffer in the beginning, but the more you persist in creating extra challenges for yourself and working through them, the more gains you will find in your learning.

It must be human nature to shy away from tasks that are difficult. We may wish to feel safe, in a zone where we know exactly what to do to get to the right answer. The problem with staying in a safe zone is that little if any learning will take place. In order to expand our learning, we have to expand our horizons and engage with interesting and tough problems in a way that challenges us. We must realize that not all difficulties are a bad thing. There is a term, **desirable difficulty**, introduced by Dr. Robert Bjork, which points to the fact that some problems that we face while learning can be beneficial. Through working with them and persisting with them, we can advance in our learning goals.

An example of a desirable difficulty could be handicapping in sports. For example, if you are a decent bowler, and you are playing against someone who is not quite as good, you should consider handicapping yourself to make the game fair. Imagine if you are an advanced bowler playing a novice. The game would be too easy and you'd have little motivation to put much effort into it. However, if you handicap yourself, giving the other player more points when they get a strike, then you have a reason to push yourself. By pushing yourself, you keep your mind active, looking for ways to improve your game and learn.

Any time you find yourself getting too comfortable with your format of learning, it's a good idea to change something that makes the learning more challenging for you. This is the kind of difficulty that is desirable and will help you meet your learning goals.

Myth #4: Fast Learning is Better than Slow Learning

It must also be a part of human nature to want things fast. We tend to want fast cars, workers who are fast, and fast learners. We appear to be in somewhat of an impatient and presumptive era, where faster is often believed to mean better. It's easy to get sucked into that belief because advertisements often flaunt and brag about their fast results. You may hear about how you can lose 10 pounds fast, perhaps in a week. Or you may hear about a speed reading course that claims to teach you to read a novel in one hour. Notice that even if the prior claims were true, they probably wouldn't claim anything about the likelihood of keeping the pounds off for the first example, or of fully understanding what was read for the second example. Speed appears to trump usefulness and long-term results, according to the advertisements. It's easy to get sucked into the hype – who wouldn't like the outcomes they claim? The problem is you have to consider that as advertisers claim faster and faster results, they end up competing with each other on speed alone. Even if the products produce legitimately fast results (which is debatable), the assumption that this is better overall may be invalid.

When it comes to learning, the notion of faster being better is flat out incorrect. The brain needs time to process what you learn, build connections, and to reflect on what has been learned. To breeze through a book, rush through homework, or perform a task as fast as possible will not lead to solid learning. In the case of learning, faster isn't always better. Those who are willing to slow down and make sure they understand concepts, how they relate to other ideas, and why they are important will be more likely to truly learn and understand.

It will be interesting to reflect that Salman Khan, the founder of Khan Academy (a free online learning center where anyone can learn mathematics, science, history, and other topics) ran a data analysis, on the performance of students who used the site. Through the site, what was emphasized was concept mastery. In normal schooling, students are advanced through to new topics whether or not they've mastered prior concepts. With the Khan Academy setup, you have to master the first concepts before getting to higher level concepts, and the amount of time taken to do this can vary between students. What he found was rather surprising. Quite often, students who breezed through earlier concepts in mathematics would slow down later as they reached advanced lessons. Also, quite often students who went slowly with earlier mathematics concepts, showing what could be assumed to be a lack of natural talent or ability, would advance faster through later lessons. Interestingly, and completely unexpectedly, the analysis showed that a student who got off to a very slow start ended up becoming the 2nd best student in the class. The student likely struggled to understand the beginning mathematical concepts, but was able to gain a solid understanding of the fundamentals and able to advance faster than others later on. This is a pattern Salman Khan has found in many classes, including different nations and socioeconomic statuses. The main point here is that just because something is learned fast early on, does not mean that this will grant an advantage over someone who starts off learning a topic slowly. We must focus on the quality of our learning over the pace at which it occurs.

Myth #5: People Learn Better when Taught According to their Particular Learning Styles

This myth has been going around for some time. It sounds logical that people would learn in different ways. The idea is that some people would learn better visually, some verbally, some analytically, some kinesthetically, and so forth. In order to reach students and teach them well, some educators and theorists believed that the students needed to be taught according to their particular styles. The key problem with this was that there was never clear evidence that teaching students according to their specific styles would help them learn better. Even if it were true that students have different learning styles (although the evidence for this isn't strong), then we still can't assume that teaching them according to their learning styles would be effective.

A big problem with the learning style theorists was that there was never much of an agreement on how many learning styles there were, or what they were. Rather than focusing on styles of learning, it may be simpler and more accurate to say that students have unique ways of learning. But overall, a teacher cannot be expected to teach to an individual style for each and every student. This approach would be too impractical, time consuming, and in the end the students wouldn't learn because none of them would get sufficient instruction.

One idea that wasn't often considered by learning style theorists is that in the real world we don't often get to choose how we learn. We are constantly taking in information through multiple modes: visual, auditory, tactile, scent, etc. Part of growing up should be to learn how to properly learn through multiple channels. It doesn't make a lot of sense to only learn through the one channel that you happen to prefer over the others. In real life we don't get that choice. Information comes at us through all angles, and it's important that we learn to process and use that information. Ultimately, we need to learn through all the modes available to us. Unless a learner has a specific disability, it will be in her best interest to continue to learn in the many ways available to her. Of course, we don't need to overwhelm ourselves by learning through multiple modes all at once. Perhaps one or two should be sufficient for any one learning task.

WHAT WE CAN LEARN FROM CHILDREN

Children aren't always seen as a great example of how to learn. Part of that reason may be that they're too young to be experts at anything yet (most of the time). However, children can actually be fantastic learners. They're naturally curious and experimental. They're not afraid of being wrong, and so they try new things enthusiastically. There are many things we can understand about learning simply through observing or studying how children learn and interact with the world around them.

The examples of children in this section will be very general. Of course, all children are different. Some are shy, some loud, some rambunctious, and some quite polite. Even though they are all unique, they do share some general characteristics. It turns out that some of those characteristics of children can be quite useful for learning. It makes sense, given that a child has a lot to learn before getting to an adult age.

Have Fun

What do children naturally want to do most of the time? Play, of course. They want to have fun, run around, go outside, go to new places and look at new things. Kids just want to have a good time. Playing, which may seem like a time waste to some adults, is actually a great way for kids to learn. They socialize with other kids, try new things, and form new experiences which help them in learning.

A reason having fun is important for learning is that there is much more engagement. There is more fascination, interest, and emotion involved, rather than idly passing the eyes over a dry textbook (although reading can be a great way to learn, but for children doing things can often be more important). As we grow older and go through the school system, we sometimes get used to learning being dry or boring. The unfortunate part of this is that many students will come to associate learning with something that is forced upon them, and not something that is enjoyable in itself. By seeking fun experiences, children learn in a more natural and enjoyable way, rather than experiencing it as something dull and unwanted.

A child who spends the day running around outside, climbing trees, falling and skinning his knees, and helping Mom make cookies will probably have learned just as much if not more in this way than by having been forced to listen to a parent lecture about the danger of climbing trees, how to put a Band-Aid on, and the steps to follow to make cookies. Why? One reason is they had fun doing it their own way, and they wanted to do it. Doing things against your will is unlikely to have as great of a learning result. The mind is likely to wander to other things that it is actually interested in, limiting the potential for learning.

As adults, obviously we don't live in the same world as children. We get used to doing things we don't want to do, as it's a normal part of life. However, we could benefit by incorporating some fun into our lives as well. We're unlikely to want to play in the same way that children do, and that's normal. The point here isn't that we should mimic children exactly in what they do. Rather, the point is that we can improve our learning by observing what children will do naturally. Children like to have fun, and they learn a lot in the process. Perhaps we could focus more on having some fun, and engaging in things we are naturally interested in, instead of pushing ourselves so hard to always learn just the things that we feel we absolutely need to know (for work or school, etc.).

Explore Widely

Many children are little explorers. They will continue to push the boundaries if allowed to do so. With their sense of wonder, they will often try new things without concern. This makes sense, after all to a young child a great many things will be new. Children actively will seek out new things. If given a new toy or a new opportunity, they will often try it out curiously, until they've figured it out.

Children don't want to be restrained. They want to seek out as many possibilities as they can. If you tell them to stay inside, they want to go out. If you tell them *not* to eat the cookies, they want to eat them. They don't like imposed limitations, just as many adults don't, and they will tend to continue exploring as much as they can until they're not allowed anymore by an adult. By wanting to explore more and widely, they open themselves up to new experiences, and more possibilities to learn something new.

Parents may notice that children seem to switch through phases rapidly. One month a child may be obsessed with Disney characters, the next month it could be Transformers. What the children are doing is rapidly learning about so many new things. It's quite possible that within just one week they will learn about something they never even knew existed. With that revelation they may become completely captivated by something new.

There is of course an important distinction between children and adults. To children, almost everything may be new. Therefore, it must be so much easier for a child to find new experiences and to explore, because almost everything is uncharted for the child. They may find new places to explore just in their own neighborhood. That is a valid point. But also, adults have many opportunities to explore new areas that they often squander. Just being an adult does not mean that someone has done it all. There are always new places to visit and new experiences to form. A child is usually limited by where his parents may take him and the areas within walking distance around their home. An adult will likely have a car or other means of transportation. Children are also limited by their reading ability. An adult on the other hand will be able to make some sense of most of the books at the book store or in the library. This presents another way to explore new fields. The point here is that adults shouldn't use the excuse that to a child everything is new. With a little bit of the exploratory mindset, adults will also realize that there are plenty of new things for them to try.

Another way to explore new areas is to seek out new friends or acquaintances. Children are often limited by their school friends, whereas adults have more freedom to meet people at work or through hobbies, or even through online channels that may help in finding friends with similar interests.

When you commit to exploring widely, you'll find that you have new information coming in from all directions. You may have an interesting conversation with a neighbor about farming. You may read a book on how robots will help humanity in 25 years. You may visit an interesting city near to your own that you had never been to and discover a rich history that you had no idea about. This kind of curiosity, openness, and willingness to explore will give you more and more information. The more we know and understand, the easier it is to learn new things. This is perhaps why children often use this strategy of constant exploration automatically.

Ask Questions

We've probably all been around a child at some point who would not stop asking questions. We have to remember that children do not have the background experience that adults have. Something an adult has seen hundreds of times may be a new and fascinating, or confusing experience for a child. The way that children begin to make sense of new experiences is to ask questions about it.

Going through the traditional school system, many of us may forget to ask questions as time passes. In school, the textbooks and teachers will ask questions of us. Even our exams will ask questions of us and we will be graded for the accuracy of our responses. Through our schooling, the questions we personally have are not seen as all that important. Rather, staying on the lesson plan and learning what is taught in the specific curriculum is what is seen as important. Through time, we ask less and less questions, as they are expected and encouraged less and less. Instead, we are often given the questions and the answers, and told to memorize them.

In reality, when you are curious and form your own questions and seek your own answers, this will provide the best environment for learning. When questions are fed to you, and the answers are conveniently available for you to find, there is a great detached feeling from the work. Really, the task will seem like busy work, and not seem personally relevant and probably will be uninteresting to you. Of course, the school system works as it does for a reason. Teachers likely find that they have better organized classrooms when they stick to a lesson plan, instead of allowing everyone to ask their own questions. That is fine, but asking your own questions and seeking your own answers will be a great learning tool, if not completely accepted inside the classroom then it should be done outside of it.

Asking questions is an important skill to have. In order to even ask a question, you first have to realize that there is something you don't know or understand. From there, a question has to be well-crafted with the intent of coming to a better understanding of a topic. It actually takes skill to come up with the right questions. A child may fall back on the often heard 'Why?', but as the child grows and asks more questions, his skill will improve and he will realize that in order to get better answers, he must ask more specific questions. The child must identify exactly what he knows and does not know, exactly what he understands and does not understand, and exactly what he is confused and not confused about. This will help for coming up with the exact question he needs to ask in order to acquire new and useful information.

As adults, we sometimes want to deny that there are things we do not know. The reality is we have just as much learning to do as a child. A child is only aware of a small amount of things that he does not know. An adult will come to realize that there are great magnitudes of things which he does not know. As adults we need to realize that there is much to learn, that we do not have all of the answers, and therefore we should take a similar strategy as that of a child. We should identify things we do not know that we'd like to know, and form questions. Even if there is not an expert on hand to ask right away, the questions are very important. Finding an expert or a forum online or the proper books from which we can seek out answers, is the easy part. The part that is absolutely essential is knowing how to form a proper question. Without the question, no one will ever give you the answer and you won't be able to search it out. The question comes first, then the search for the proper tools or resources to answer it, and then finally the answer may come. Of course, more complicated or challenging questions can take longer to solve, but that's a part of the process.

Experiment

Jean Piaget was a developmental psychologist, well known for his theories on how children's minds develop. As a brief overview, he stated that there are four key stages that children go through in their development. In the **sensorimotor stage** (birth to 24 months) infants are mostly focused on sensations they get from their bodies. In the **pre-operational stage** (24 months to 7 years) children are beginning to process symbols such as words and images, but they aren't quite able to use them in a meaningful way yet. In the **concrete operations stage** (7 to 12 years) children are able to use symbols in a meaningful way, but only concretely such as for physical objects. In the **formal operations stage** (12 years and up), children are able to think abstractly. They can think about concepts that are not concrete, such as love or the future.

In the sensorimotor stage, Piaget was known to think of children as 'little scientists'. Of course, they wouldn't engage in all of the technicalities that a true scientist would, but the idea was that young children were constantly observing and testing their environment. They were likely forming a basic picture of the physical rules that all people and things are governed by. For example, a young child may play with her toys, and to an adult it can appear like mindless play. However, to the child, bouncing a rubber ball can be a discovery that shows soft things that feel rubbery can bounce. Then if the child throws it harder, she may notice that the ball bounces farther and with more force. A child will appear to be testing how the world around her works, and coming to conclusions based on those tests. That process must be what Piaget meant when he described children in the sensorimotor stage as little scientists.

As we grow older, we won't be interested in the sorts of tests or experiments that children perform. However, that experimental, testing, and exploratory approach can be quite useful for learning. In order to have a good chance of learning something new, you must try something new. A young child in the sensorimotor stage may do silly things like try to bounce a ball off of the floor, a wall, and a couch. Then the child may put the ball in his mouth. As silly as it seems, these are all learning experiences. The child is learning that rubber balls bounce pretty well off of a hard floor, they also bounce off of walls but in a different way, and they don't bounce much off of a couch. Also, he will learn that a rubber ball isn't food and doesn't taste very good.

An adult who wants to experiment, rather than play with toys, may try out new tools for learning. For example, you may try new computer or phone applications to see if they help your productivity at work. You could try learning how the program works, then use it for a week or a month and then check if your productivity has gone up as a result of using it. A lot of experimentation can be viewed more simply, as a process of trial and error.

Be Willing to Make Mistakes

Often, children are more than willing to make mistakes. They may often be unaware of the potential consequences of their actions, and so therefore be more than willing to dive headfirst into a challenging problem. Children, like adults, can of course become worried about making mistakes and failing, but this is something that happens as children get a little older and more experienced, and unfortunately they may have even had adults criticize them for their errors.

Some scientists such as B. F. Skinner (a prominent behaviorist in the 1960s and 70s) believed that making errors was to be avoided at all costs. They had a theory that when you make a mistake, you would learn that mistake instead of the correct way to perform a task, and therefore you would continue to make that mistake over and over. This theory led to studies that were designed with the purpose to prevent errors from happening while learning. Finally, with these new studies there was the beginning of a revelation: when students were prevented from making errors while learning, they performed *worse*, not better. Researchers such as Dr. Michael Frese have conducted studies supporting that an environment which allows for and even encourages errors to take place will cultivate and stimulate learning. The important part is to focus on learning from those errors, rather than worrying about seeing them as something to be avoided.

When learning something new, children will of course make mistakes. While playing with Legos, they may not follow the instructions properly, or they put pieces together haphazardly, resulting in constructions that don't make any sense in the real world. They may sometimes be unaware that a mistake has even taken place, especially among younger children. The phase that is more interesting, however, is when children are old enough to make mistakes and to realize that they have made one. You will observe that they seek out a way to correct the mistake they've made. If the example is Legos, and the child noticed that he has designed an object that doesn't make sense, he may go back to the instruction sheet and try to find where his design took a different direction than what the instructions state. This is how learning occurs. The next time the child constructs something with Legos, the child is unlikely to make as big of a mistake. As the child continues to use Legos and follow the instructions, he will improve and learn from any little mistakes that occur, making those same mistakes less and less often.

The above example may seem simple and obvious. Of course, the more we do a task and perform errors, and try to correct them, the more we will improve at the task and therefore make those errors less and less often. Well, if it's so obvious, you would think that more people would see errors as an aid for greater learning, rather than as something to be avoided at all costs. What often happens is that it is human nature to immediately notice mistakes and point them out, especially in other people. But it usually doesn't feel good to have your own mistakes pointed out. A person may even feel personally attacked, like there is something wrong with him for having made a mistake. Of course, we should avoid feeling personally attacked for our errors, and we should avoid making others feel that way. If someone ever points out an error that you make, thank them and tell them you are glad you've been made aware of it so you can now begin to learn and improve. It's easy to point out mistakes in others, but in order to learn we have to recognize and work on our prior mistakes.

Simply recall that the goal of learning isn't to prevent future errors. A key goal of learning, however, is to learn from the errors you commit. It's important to stop and reexamine the problem when you do make a mistake, and consider how you can fix it. We'll never be perfect, and we shouldn't necessarily try to. Making mistakes and trying to correct them is a key part of the learning process.

Be Imaginative and Creative

Children will sometimes become completely absorbed with play, but the interesting thing is that at a young age they don't need toys in order to play. Children may play a game of 'House' from a very young age, where they pretend to be a family, with several children playing a different role, such as mother, father, child, etc. What children do often and what they are good at is pretending. If they like a cartoon or a movie, they might have fun pretending to play the role of the hero. Something else they may do is play a game where the good guys (cops) have to chase the bad guys (robbers).

Unfortunately as children grow older, they tend to become less creative and imaginative. Part of this may have to do with a school system that does appear to encourage creativity and imagination less and less. It's common to hear about schools closing or reducing budgets for their arts and music programs, for example. Also, schools are reducing outside recreational play, which may have been a good time for children to exercise their imaginations as well.

As we grow older we won't be interested in the same kind of pretend play as children. However, there are many other ways to exercise our creativity and imagination. We may pick up a creative hobby such as painting or drawing. We may write a short story or make up a bedtime story for a child. There are many ways to be creative and there is no strict rule or way to go about it. If you are interested in machines you might try to design one of your own. If you like computers, you might learn how to program and try to design your own program. With technology now, there are more and more ways to create. For example, there are now computer programs that are built to help you create your own digital music. You don't even need to learn to play an instrument. Of course, learning to use these programs to create music may be equally challenging, but the point is there are many options available to those who are motivated.

In order to be creative, and to make something new, will require a lot of learning and effort. You will have to decide what the purpose is, and work toward meeting that end goal. There are often limitations such as time, money, or other materials, and part of the creative process is finding a way to accomplish your goals with what you have, or finding a way to get more of those resources if you need them.

One of the great things about engaging in a creative or imaginative project of some sort is that this kind of learning brings together other great learning strategies. Creativity brings a synthesis of many critical components of learning. For example, most people associate creative tasks with fun. When having fun, as was already stated, you'll be more motivated, more engaged, and more likely to actually learn. Through the creative process you'll also likely need to ask yourself many questions in order to advance yourself to a higher level in your abilities or in your progress on your projects. Also, as you try to achieve your goals, you will probably need to experiment with different materials or different processes to see if you can meet the desired results. When engaging in creative projects, you are likely to be delving into uncharted territory. At some point you will just need to try things out and see what happens.

Finally, when you open yourself up to trying new things and engaging in uncertain and creative projects, it is entirely possible that you will commit errors. That is fine, as one of the best paths to learning is in learning from your mistakes. We've all made mistakes we regretted, but I am sure you would agree that the biggest mistakes you've ever made are fully ingrained into your memories, and they are mistakes you would never make again. Well, one definition of learning is actually when you have made a lasting change in your behavior. If errors can lead to this, then they are a great tool for learning. The main thing to keep in mind is to control the kind of errors you make. Allow yourself some freedom to make errors that are unlikely to be too costly or disastrous. Don't make errors on purpose, but when they happen, allow yourself to learn and move on.

For these reasons, engaging in your own creative projects will likely be a great learning opportunity. Creative projects will involve a great synthesis of learning. If you want to advance yourself in a specific topic, one of the best things you can do to propel your learning, knowledge, and expertise forward, is to initiate a creative project of your own.

THE LEARNING PROCESS

By reading this book, I presume you want to improve your own learning skills and abilities. In order to do so it makes sense to have a good general understanding of how the learning process works. For now, you may have a simple model in your mind of how learning works. If you want to learn about cars, for example, you may buy a book or Google the topic. That is a very sensible approach, but in this section we will cover more of the specifics of what needs to happen in order to learn. For example, even reading itself is an activity that is different for different people. Two people can read the same book and come away with different levels of comprehension. It's important to know how we form meaning and understanding. Everyone knows that reading is helpful for acquiring information, but this section will deal more with how we may truly make sense of that information and use it to learn more deeply.

Learning is a process, and no two learning events will be the same. Also, no two people will learn in the same way. In recognizing this, it isn't an easy thing to come up with an overall learning process. The reality is that the process will be uniquely different depending on the person and topic. Nonetheless, there are some general similarities among most learning that takes place. The following section will show the process of learning across all kinds of domains. Also, it will start from the beginning and move on to more advanced learning concepts. It will assume no prior knowledge of whatever the topic is that you may want to learn. As you read about this learning process, feel free to imagine any topic area you wish. You could imagine how it applies to learning to play drums, to understanding physics, or to becoming a teacher, for example.

Every single part of this overall process will not be essential for everything you want to learn. This section should not be viewed as a checklist for learning. How many parts of the process are needed will depend on what you want to learn, your level of prior experience in the topic, and just how deeply you wish to learn something. For most kinds of learning, you may only engage in a few of the parts laid out here. However, if you want to truly master a topic, and fully learn it, you may very well use most or all of the parts of this learning process.

This learning process includes what I believe are the most important and essential features of learning. The specific components of this process are based in sound research. Rather than including every single aspect of learning that is known, as there may be hundreds, I have included those that are most essential, important, and relevant to a wide range of fields.

Know your Motivation and Purpose

Perhaps your motivation and purpose are the same thing, but if you are preparing yourself for a long journey of learning about an entire domain, or a large portion of a field, or embarking on gaining an entire new skill, it helps to have a true understanding of your motivations. It can be helpful to have more than just one, actually. Some motivations may be to acquire a skill that can help you earn more income, to satisfy a lifelong urge to learn about a topic, to help people who struggle with a specific problem that you will learn to solve, etc.

It is possible that your motivation may be small. Perhaps you are in a class where a teacher assigned some homework. If you're not interested in the task, your sole motivation may be to get a decent grade so you can pass or do well in the course and later get a job. This level of motivation may be good enough to get you through a small learning goal, but not a larger one.

When you want to learn something that is more ambitious, you should question your motivation. It will help to come up with many reasons why you want to achieve a particular goal, or many reasons why you are so motivated that you wouldn't give up so easily. Sooner or later, if you wish to learn something that is challenging and ambitious, you will come across a task or a challenge that appears overwhelmingly difficult. At that point it will seem easier just to give up and let it go. You can save yourself some trouble by having a strong understanding of your motivations early on. If you really know why you're committed to a learning goal, then when faced with a difficulty, your decision will be an easy one – to push through and keep doing your best, because you have specific reasons for wanting to learn the material.

When you have your motivation decided, you can then move on to figuring out your detailed purpose. First, you will decide what topic you want to learn. Then, you will ask yourself *why* you want to learn it. Your *why* or your reason, is your purpose. Depending on your purpose for learning, you should figure out to what depth or to what specificity you should learn this topic for your goals.

For example, someone who wishes to change their car battery on their own may be fine with learning simply about car batteries, how to change them, and any tools needed to do so. On the other hand, someone who wishes to learn how a car works in general, so they can make sure that they understand all of their costs at the car dealership, and so they can take care of minor problems on their own, will want to engage in much more in depth learning. This person may read books or take a course, practice changing their oil, changing their own battery, and replacing minor parts on their vehicle as needed.

It's important to know your purpose for learning so you can decide to what extent you need to learn. This is a matter of efficiency. Some kinds of learning projects will be fairly quick, where you can meet your goals in a few days perhaps, and other learning goals may require substantial time and effort.

Your motivation and purpose are both important for meeting your learning goals. You will want to be sure to identify them for yourself before you begin a large learning project. To skip this part can lead to issues further down the line. If you do make the mistake of skipping this step, you may find that your motivations for learning a topic were rather weak. Or you may find that your purpose wasn't well thought out. Perhaps there was an easier topic you could have learned to meet your goals.

For example, someone who wants to repair computers does not need to get a computer engineering degree. It would be a more direct path to seek actual experience in working with computers, and perhaps to seek out other certifications for that specific goal. An engineering degree would focus on a lot of areas that aren't necessary for repairing a computer, and therefore be an inefficient use of time for the intended goal.

Identify Key Terms, Concepts, and Rules

In order to begin learning something new, you need to become well versed in the language. This can include both formal terminology and informal lingo that is used among those who work in the field. An example of formal terms used in poker would be that the pool of money all the players are trying to win is called 'the pot', and the first three cards that are laid out for all players to see and play with is called 'the flop'. As far as informal lingo goes, expert players in poker are sometimes called 'sharks', and new or poor players are sometimes referred to as 'fish'. It's important to begin learning terms such as these when you want to learn in a new topic so that you can communicate with experts, and so that you can begin to make sense of important concepts.

Let's take this idea a bit further, because sometimes it is just as important if not more so to understand rule structures. For example, in algebra, it will be important of course to identify key terms and concepts, just like with any other field. You'll want to learn what the common symbols are, such as '+' means plus, '±' means plus or minus, and '≠' means not equal to. Of course, there are many other important symbols such as exponents and so forth. But with a rule-based system like algebra, it will also be important to learn general rules. Some of those rules may be in the form of formulas, such as the quadratic formula. In order to perform any operations with the formula, first you must know it. Also, order of operations should be known, PEMDAS, parentheses, exponents, multiplication, division, addition, then subtraction. This is the order that an equation must be worked out in.

If you're not learning algebra, or interested in it, don't worry. What you should realize is that in order to learn some fields, especially very rule-based fields like mathematics, it will be important to learn both concepts and the specific rules that govern the field. If you fail to learn these things, you will constantly find that you misunderstand something. Often students are either pushed to advance too quickly, or they impatiently push themselves to advance too quickly, and they end up having gaps in their knowledge. It's silly to be working on advanced theoretical ideas in a topic when there isn't even a mastery of the basic concepts, ideas, definitions, and rule structures that operate in a field. Discover what those are, with the help of an expert if needed, and take the time to fully understand and memorize them if needed, and you will be in a good position later to excel.

Prioritize the most important elements

This idea follows directly from the prior section of identifying key terms, concepts, and rules. When you've gone ahead and identified them, you may find yourself overwhelmed. Perhaps there are hundreds, thousands, or even more of these concepts. Rather than committing to learning everything all at once, it's important to prioritize what is most essential or foundational to learn first. If some concepts are important to understand, or more relevant, or more common in some way, then focus on those first.

The challenge is that as a novice, if you are one, it may be difficult to determine this for yourself. If you are in fact a novice, seek out some kind of instruction from an expert. You don't necessarily need to pay for a tutor or take a class, although those things would certainly help. With some searching online, you may find a professor's syllabus, outlining what they think is most important to know. Or you may find an encyclopedia page or some other blog or resource that lays out what a particular expert believes is especially important. You should be careful however, that not all learning materials are designed for someone new to the field. You must continue to search until you find a listing of concepts that makes sense to you, and that is meant for a novice to begin learning in the field. At this point, it is unnecessary to concern yourself with advanced concepts or topics that rely on a foundation first. This is the point where you acquire your foundation, so you can later make sense of those more advanced topics.

An example of prioritizing the most important elements or concepts, is if you were to imagine learning a new language. In order to simplify this example, let's ignore the grammar side of language for a moment, and assume that as a beginning goal you want to learn some vocabulary. How do you define the most important words to know? You could do this in different ways. If you want to work professionally in a new language, you could focus on key words that you use in your field, and learn those in the new language. Another way to identify the most important words is simply to begin with the most commonly spoken words and phrases. There should be websites or perhaps books you can find to help you with this. Most of the time when we speak or write, we use many of the same words over and over. By focusing on the most important elements, the words and phrases that reoccur, you will make the best use of your time.

When you have learned these most important elements, you will be in a much better position to begin putting together grammar and learning new words. Remember, first you should master the basics, and then move on. Do not rush it. If you have failed to understand something on a basic level, you will later find yourself frustrated, and likely be forced to return to the basics to relearn them before you can move forward.

Connect Information Together

It's important to relate what you learn to your prior experiences or to other phenomena. As an example, there are roughly 100 billion neurons in the brain, and roughly 100 billion stars in the Milky Way galaxy. This is a connection, relating different pieces of information.

Why is connecting information together in a meaningful way important? The mind doesn't work well with isolated facts that build no connection. As an example, how can the average person make sense of the stars in the sky at night? It seems incomprehensible that someone could make any sense of it, or remember them without some kind of meaning behind them. Although most of us today wouldn't be particularly concerned with learning deeply about the stars, it was essential that our ancestors learn them. They used them for navigation and for knowing when seasons were going to change. Using the stars for these purposes was important for survival, important for managing their lives and gave them a greater understanding of the world around them.

So, how did our ancestors make sense of these random bright dots (the stars) up in the sky? Rather than look at them as isolated dots, they saw them as interconnected. Our ancestors saw figures in the stars such as Osiris, an Egyptian God of the afterlife. They built stories around these figures. Some of them were good, some were bad, some were strong and some were weak and needed protection. Stories are a good way of connecting information too. Our ancestors may have been smarter than some of us would give them credit for. They used sound learning practices to learn the stars. And they used sound teaching practices too, because by linking the stars together into grand images, and telling stories around them, they insured that the children and young adults of their time would also learn the stars, increasing their odds of survival.

In connecting information together, the most important goal is to build an understanding. Memorization has a place in learning (such as when learning concepts and rules), but when we simply memorize we may not truly understand the information, because we haven't necessarily taken the time to connect it in a way that makes sense.

There are many ways that we can connect new information that we are learning with prior information we've already absorbed. If you think about it, something everyone has is prior personal experiences. Whether you have experience working at a specific job, growing up in the city, as a member of a debate team, or any other unique experiences you've acquired in life, these are experiences that are completely ingrained as a part of you. They make sense to you because you've lived through them. Therefore, when you're learning something new if you can find a way to relate the material to your prior life experiences, you will find that this connection makes your learning much more reliable. Relating back to your personal experiences can sometimes be a stretch, especially with more abstract concepts, or with ideas that seem to have no relationship to your life. If you search hard enough, though, you may find some kind of link, and that link can help you remember and understand the new information you're trying to acquire.

Practice and Apply

In order to truly learn something, you must *do it.* For example, someone can read many books and receive many lectures on how to be a good grade school teacher. They may learn about child behavior, classroom management, and master the concepts that children need to learn to do well. However, learning about teaching, and the reality of teaching must be different things.

Children are known to be somewhat unpredictable. They may do things that were not mentioned in any classes on how to teach. Perhaps they aren't as obedient as would have been assumed, or they don't learn as fast or pay attention as much as was assumed in the classes on how to teach. Teaching, as with many other skills, is something that must be practiced in a real classroom in order to truly advance ones learning.

It may seem that teaching is unique, and so of course you need to practice the skill in order to really learn it, but there are countless other disciplines where it's important to practice the skill in order to have a good grasp on it. In fact, as a general rule, anything that is considered a skill will likely need to be practiced in order to learn it on a deep level. For example, how can someone really know Spanish or French if they never speak it?

This step in the learning process does not just apply to skills, however. Even when learning from a book or in a topic that is not a skill, we'll be better in our learning if we seek to apply the content in some way. You may apply it simply by discussing it with a fellow student or a friend. If you're reading classic fiction, like Leo Tolstoy for example, you may apply your knowledge of the book by discussing it with a friend. You may discuss the characters, the setting of the book, and the history and politics that took place.

For the most part, many people are aware that practice is important to learning. But the key isn't simply practicing, but in how we practice as well. There is a common saying that 'practice makes perfect', but it isn't fully true. We must learn to practice effectively, in order for it to truly pay off.

Many people will spend time practicing skills inefficiently. Although it can be enjoyable to just practice the fun parts of a skill, this is unlikely to be the way that will enable you to learn the most. For example, focusing too much on practicing dunking in basketball won't be as useful as practicing more important areas of the game, or areas in which a particular player is weak. Also, practicing just the fun or easy parts of a song on piano will not be as efficient as practicing the more difficult areas and the areas that give a player trouble.

There is a term, **deliberate practice**, which is important to be aware of. This is a term originated and heavily researched by psychologist Anders Ericsson. Something to understand is that people who achieve expertise in a skill tend to get there by the way they practice. Although natural talent may play a role in someone's accomplishments, something that we actually have control over is *how we practice*. More practice isn't necessarily optimal, but how we practice is what truly matters. Of course what deliberate practice means exactly will change from skill to skill, and even person to person depending on what stage of learning they are in.

Deliberate practice has been found to be the best way to practice to efficiently acquire expertise. Idle practice is not the key to learning and improvement. It must be active, purposeful, and guided in a specific direction that is meant to improve one's skill. It's more important to pay attention to weaknesses, feedback, and critical areas that must be mastered in order to make progress, rather than on the hours spent practicing. Deliberate practice involves enough challenge that it will be important to have a tutor or adviser, especially for the novice who finds it difficult to judge their weaknesses, strengths, and where they must focus to make the most progress.

Another important concept when it comes to practice, is that you should **practice like you play**. In other words, practice as you would in the final environment where you are expected to perform your skill. Practicing like you play will be most critical for anyone performing a skill that could be dangerous, such as pilots and police officers, but it's also important for others as well.

In this regard, think about how pilots learn to fly. They learn in highly advanced simulators that are meant to simulate every single aspect of flying. When a pilot is flying a commercial plane, he is expected to go through a checklist of everything that must be completed before the flight takes off. Usually the pilot will be aware of everything on the checklist, and may not even feel that he needs it in order to do his job. However, the checklist is a safety precaution that must be used by all commercial pilots. A pilot in training may decide that it's silly to follow a checklist for a simulated flight when he already knows what to do. However, such behavior on a true flight can be hazardous. Imagine failing to notice that the gasoline tank lacks fuel on a real flight!

Unfortunately, a pilot who neglects practicing going through the checklist during simulation is more likely to forget to do it when the time comes to fly in a real aircraft, jeopardizing his career and the safety of those on board. As you can see, when someone is practicing a skill, he should seek to do it in as similar of an environment as he can to the actual one he'll be expected to do it in. And he should do it in the same way he'll need to it in a true situation. To neglect this principle can have disastrous consequences.

Seek out Feedback

Without some form of feedback, it can be difficult to improve in your abilities and learning. Feedback will be most important when learning a skill, such as Tennis, Chess, or a language, but feedback is also important in book learning too.

The best persons to get feedback from will be teachers and experts, or really anyone who has a substantial amount of knowledge in the topic over you. In order to improve, it will be essential to become aware of what your weaknesses and strengths are. An expert will be able to tell you what your problem areas are, and will also be able to show you how you can make progress.

The problem with *not* seeking feedback is that it's easy to become overconfident in your skills without it. You may think you are progressing quite well and doing a great job, but in reality you could be making a terrible mistake. And worse yet, you may be making that same mistake over and over because you're unaware of it.

Aside from seeking **expert feedback**, it can also be useful to consider **system feedback**. This means getting feedback from the system in which you're working. For example, when working with computer programs, if something is done incorrectly it's common to get either an error or an alert of some kind. This would be feedback you're getting from the system itself. It's telling you that you did something wrong and you should fix it. Microsoft word, for example, gives simple feedback if you do a spelling/grammar check. It will alert you to spelling mistakes and simple grammar issues. Through this feedback, you can improve the quality of your writing.

Expert feedback is often more detailed and helpful to your specific needs. System feedback can be a bit difficult to figure out, or it may not tell you exactly what you need to do to fix the problem. Often times, with system feedback you will simply be alerted that what you tried to do did not work. For example, if you try to print off a page and your printer doesn't print it out correctly, then that is also system feedback. It's very basic because all it tells you is that it didn't work, but it is still feedback.

Some professionals, such as computer programmers, will become quite expert at dealing with system feedback. They will design a program, run it, and then check through pages of feedback or error messages to verify if every part of the program is working correctly. It can take many years of expertise and practice for a programmer to effectively use detailed system feedback to make corrections to her program. For most people, expert feedback will be simpler, and the preferred option. System feedback can be used as a secondary source of information that will also be useful to share with an expert.

We've discussed **expert feedback** and **system feedback**, but there are other forms of feedback as well. You may get **feedback from peers** or clients/users. Peers are just fellow learners who may be at the same level as you, and who may share their opinions and feedback with you. Of course, since peers are roughly at the same level as you, you have to be cautious about blindly accepting their feedback. You should consider and evaluate the feedback, especially if the peer is well-respected and a hard worker. And if you are working with an expert, you may mention the feedback you've gotten from peers. Usually, the expert will have more experience and will be in a better position to tell you what you really need to work on.

Feedback from clients or users, on the other hand, comes into play when you have designed some sort of product or even a process that others will use. In that case, someone (a client or user) will try out what you have created. You may not have access to clients or their feedback, but if you do, you can get a unique impression from such users. She will have a lot of interest in how the product you've created works. Every client may have her own unique tastes, but if a client finds issues that are very basic, or big flaws, these will be very important for you to learn from. Imagine, for example that you are a novice painter, and you sell one of your creations to a client. That client loves the painting and she has a tremendous respect for your work. However, after a year of owning the painting, she calls you, devastated, stating that the painting is showing signs of deterioration. It turns out that when you created the painting, you accidentally used poor quality materials. In that case it would be important to make sure that you corrected your mistake going into the future.

However, if a client mentions that she does not like your painting because the style is too old-fashioned, then you need to consider your own goals. Is the client correct that your painting appears old fashioned? If she is, were you going for that sort of style? If you were, and you were meeting your goals, then you can take into account the client's feedback, but everyone has a separate taste and in the end you need to keep your goals in mind.

Peer and client/user feedback should both be used with some caution. They can be valuable and helpful, but due to the fact that peers and clients are usually not experts, or aware of everything that goes into making good quality work, you can't always blindly accept the feedback. At the same time, you should not blindly disregard such feedback either. Someone who seems like a peer may actually have many years of extra experience over you. Also, a client may be a great fan of the products you create and be well informed about what makes them good quality. To completely disregard such a client could be a great mistake.

Reflect on your Learning and Find General Principles

At the end of the day, or after you've engaged in your learning activities, the act of learning is not finished. It is still important to reflect back on what you have learned. This step in the learning process may share many characteristics with prior ones, but this step should be seen as important but still separate from the prior steps. The prior steps will be a part of your main learning experience. They will happen while you actively work on a task, practice it, and seek to improve your abilities based on any feedback you gain in the process. Reflection will occur later, when you are likely no longer engaging in actively learning the material or practicing the task you wish to learn.

It's good to sometimes give yourself some separation from the learning task. This way, you can reflect and calmly think back to how your learning is going. You may think about the task itself. Is there some connection you've missed? Is there something important you need to understand that has escaped you? Is what you are trying to learn much tougher than you originally thought, and it will actually require much more effort on your part? Or is it much easier than you expected, and since you expect to master it soon you should consider if you'd like to focus on learning something different later?

The reflecting stage of learning is guided heavily by questions, as you may have noticed. The questions will change depending on what you want to learn, and they will also change depending on what your focus is and what you consider important in your learning.

Note that reflecting on your own is usually quite useful. It's good to form your own opinions and observation of how your learning is going. But it's perfectly fine and useful to share your reflections with someone else. In this sense, you can use your thoughts and reflections as a tool to help get guided feedback to make your learning go more efficiently. Also, if you need someone else to bounce ideas off of to help you reflect, then that is perfectly fine.

A good tool to help with reflecting is using notes. If you take your learning seriously, it can make sense to have a designated notepad or file on your computer where you diligently keep track of your thoughts on your progress, and what you could do to improve. If you find some domain, skill, or topic that you are completely committed to, and to which you'd like to dedicate your life to and become a master in, it could make great sense to keep a running log of your progress and thoughts.

Some other questions you can ask yourself are: What is the grand overarching theme of what I'm learning? Instead of getting so focused on miniscule details, what is the big picture? Also, what are the key principles and takeaways from what I've learned? Try to determine general rules or characteristics that apply to your whole domain. How would you explain what you've learned to someone who doesn't know the topic? Someone who truly knows a topic should be able to fluidly explain it to someone else. Don't get concerned if you can't explain all of a domain to someone else. Instead, pick a part of the domain. Pick a subtopic, or pick what you're learning at the moment, and consider how you could explain it to a layperson.

To truly know a topic, you should search deep and discover the underlying principles, the kernels of truth and mine them out of your life experiences. Experiencing stuff, doing stuff, and seeing stuff isn't enough. You have to interpret the meaning of it all, and what it means to your life, for yourself.

Synthesize: Internalize, Integrate, and Organize

Now, we reach the final stage of learning. This is an advanced form of learning that not everyone will concern themselves with. It's not an essential part of learning, in that you can learn quite a bit and make great progress without ever getting to this stage. Also, it's possible to engage in synthesizing your learning without having fully gone through all the prior stages. Just because you have taken it upon yourself to engage in synthesis does not necessarily mean you are a complete master of your chosen domain.

In this stage of learning, there are many things that can happen. One scenario is that you completely **internalize** what you have learned. You've come to a point of mastery, where it feels like a certain domain is a part of you. Perhaps you've studied it so much that you have an intuitive and seemingly natural grasp of the topic. You may have studied and engaged with a topic for so many years that you effortlessly see analogies between this domain and every other aspect of your life. It's almost a challenge not to think of your domain, because you've internalized it so much. It has become a part of you.

Imagine a successful therapist who has helped people improve their psychological conditions over 20 years. Whenever she notices some kind of interpersonal conflict, or a personal issue in someone she knows, it's likely that she may automatically jump into a mode of thinking about the issues through her prior training. Also, someone who has excelled to a high level of mathematics and who solves challenging problems on a daily basis may come to see expressions of mathematical ideas and equations in the everyday life around him. A soccer ball may call to mind equations for the volume of a sphere. He may run statistical calculations of probabilities in his mind for the everyday decisions he makes in his life. Everywhere he goes, math follows. He has internalized math concepts, and they are a part of him.

Another thing that happens at this stage is **integration**. After enough time learning and mastering one field, sometimes a person will learn and master another field as well. When having a solid understanding of two fields, a person will be much more likely to integrate her understanding to a level where she sees more and more links between topics. In some fields, this level of merging is seen commonly, such as with biochemistry, the integration of biology and chemistry. However, it could just as easily occur with other unique fields. When someone masters two fields, it becomes more likely to find more and more connections among the two areas.

Through novel integrations, new fields can be created or discovered. It becomes possible for new technologies or processes to be created that unite different fields. Bioinformatics, for example, is a union of biological information and using computers to measure and use biological information more efficiently.

In order to achieve a deep and informed level of integration, you must deliberately and attentively build your knowledge and understanding of one topic. When that one topic is mastered, you can begin pursuing mastery in another topic. Of course, you could pursue learning in two topics at once, it just may take longer to achieve mastery this way. Whichever way you choose to proceed, as you pursue understanding in both domains, you will begin to see more and more connections between them. This process will involve some deep thought, deep elaboration, and reflection, all of the things that have been discussed in the prior stages of learning. A true integration, or a deep understanding between two or more fields, will be the height of learning. Not many people will achieve it, but those who do will likely experience great breakthroughs and insights.

Organization is a key part of building a synthesis of understanding. When learning, at first we learn concepts in isolation. We may memorize definitions of them. As time passes, we see interrelationships between concepts, and we start to understand how they work together. After some time of building more and more relationships in our minds, and beginning to get a grasp of the big picture, it's important that we establish an organization of all of the information we have in a topic. Without a good organization in our understanding, we can still get lost in details.

Of course, in time we may naturally come to organize everything in our minds. But we can do something to speed up this process, to enable a deeper understanding. We can organize what we understand on paper or on a computer, in physical form that we can observe and modify. There are many ways to organize information. For example, we can structure information via outlines, concept maps, diagrams, tables, charts, maps, etc. Sometimes we just form a jumble of isolated links or ideas in the mind, and we don't know how it *all* works together. Some fields can become quite complex. Even a single model in your domain may be loaded with complexity. It would be your choice if you want to make separate models for yourself to help understand many different parts of your field. But it also may be useful to create one great overarching model that encompasses the entire field. As difficult and unfathomable as it may be, to do so could be quite useful to ensure that you have a good organizational understanding of your domain.

LESS EFFECTIVE WAYS TO LEARN

Before we jump in to some useful and effective ways to be a better learner, it would make sense first to cover some commonly used but less effective ways of learning that many students and learners engage in. Just as there are many myths to learning, there are also many less effective ways of learning that people get used to. It's easy to fall into old habits. And if you achieve a good result even through a poor learning technique, you may feel that your poor learning technique was helpful when it really wasn't. This is a fairly common mistake, so let's cover some of these less effective ways of learning.

The following techniques are not necessarily ineffective or useless, but they are generally less effective than more useful techniques which will be introduced in the next section. John Dunlosky and his fellow researchers have reviewed 10 major learning techniques. Their review supports that the following learning techniques are generally less effective. But remember that every individual is different. It seems possible that some people will find a way to learn well even with a technique that isn't useful for most people. Or an individual may have taken the time to modify one of these less effective techniques in order to make it much more effective. Given these possibilities, I'll refrain from stating that any technique is all bad. Rather, this section should serve as a warning, that for most people, according to research, these techniques will be limited in their usefulness, and it should pay off more to use a proven effective learning technique.

Highlighting and Underlining

If you ask any student how they study and prepare for exams, you'll find that many of them feel highlighting and underlining their texts is a good way to help them learn. The research has spoken on this, however, and it is *not* a very effective way to learn. An issue with highlighting your texts is that you may come to focus too much on specific facts, rather than building an overall understanding of how everything fits together.

Even still, highlighting may be helpful in certain cases. Perhaps you want to be sure that you note some very important passages, so you can look at them later and think about them, and make deeper connections among other important passages. This could be a useful way of highlighting. However, often times when people do highlight, they do so passively, finding important material and continuing to move on in their reading without actively processing it. Also, as you read it may be difficult to know for sure what is truly important. Perhaps a true understanding of what is most important and what is trivial or background material will become more obvious *after* reading a chapter or section of a book. But of course people tend to highlight while they read, not after.

Rereading

Another very popular way to learn material, especially for students, will be rereading the same texts or notes multiple times. Often, if something feels like work, and we spend a lot of time going through the process, we expect it to pay off. Rereading feels like work, and it feels like something should come out of it. Surely, there are some benefits that come from rereading, but for the time investment, the gains are minimal. Unfortunately, this technique is not as helpful as many of us would think.

It may make sense to reread a particularly challenging passage that wasn't well understood the first time. But to reread an entire chapter, or an entire set of notes may not be especially helpful. By rereading an entire chapter, an equal amount of time is being spent across more difficult areas and easier areas, parts that were well understood and parts that weren't, and so forth. Also, in reading, we tend to feel that we understand the material as we are reading it. It makes sense at the time, but later on when we are tested, that's when we feel that we didn't quite grasp something. The act of rereading doesn't challenge us, and can in fact bore us. Through that lack of challenge we are likely to misunderstand, forget, and ultimately waste time.

Summarizing

Of course, a summary is simply writing a shorter version of a passage of text, aiming to capture the most important parts in the learners own words. Some students or learners will summarize important texts or notes that they've acquired in hopes of learning the material. Does it work? Yes and no. It turns out that summarizing is itself a skill. Younger students will tend not to be very good at it yet. Older students, especially of college age or older, will be more capable of creating a useful summary. This matters because when a learner is able to create a good summary that is accurate and captures the important parts, she will be much more likely to benefit in her learning from the summary.

The support for summarization is actually somewhat mixed. This could be for many reasons. As mentioned above, how good the student is at summarizing matters. The research also isn't definitive on whether long or short summaries are better, whether summarizing is more useful at the paragraph or chapter level, if it's more useful for certain kinds of content, or how exactly a summary should be prepared in order for it to be beneficial. Studies have shown, however, that summarizing is more effective for learning than simply taking verbatim notes. It's also better to summarize in efforts to learn rather than not summarizing or doing anything else at all.

The bottom line is that summarization as a technique for learning is better than doing nothing, and it is more useful for older students or learners who have had some practice in summarizing effectively. However, summarizing is not as effective as some other more helpful techniques. Someone who wishes to be a skilled learner will probably avoid this technique for learning unless their learning goals would be benefited from learning to summarize in itself, rather than for other ends. For example, if you are learning to teach young students, it could be useful to learn to summarize more difficult concepts so you can explain them better to your students. Also, if you would like to be a journalist, this may involve paraphrasing and summarizing frequently, so it could be a useful skill to practice. But summarizing is not likely to be the most useful technique for learning in general.

Multi-tasking

Many students or learners feel quite comfortable with a range of technology. They're very used to television, smart phones, tablets, computers, and other electronic devices that use up our attention. They're very comfortable with them, and can sometimes forget that everything you do will take up some attention.

When learning something new, one of the worst things you can do is attempt to do other tasks at the same time. Whether they're chores, for entertainment, or you're trying to learn two things at once, your performance will be worse for attempting to multi-task. When we begin to learn something, it needs our full attention. Without that attention, it's easy to engage with the task passively, idly taking in information, only later to realize that very little was learned or understood.

There have been studies that show people are generally not good at multi-tasking. Interestingly enough, a study by researcher David Sanbonmatsu and his colleagues shows that people who think they are better multi-taskers actually tend to be the worst at it. This sounds similar to the Dunning-Kruger effect, doesn't it, where less skilled people overestimate their abilities, and more skilled people underestimate them.

We have to realize that when we do multi-task, we aren't dividing our attention equally between two things. We are actually shifting our attention back and forth across different areas. And each time you shift your attention, you lose efficiency. Of course, this may not be an issue for someone doing two easy tasks that are already learned, such as folding laundry and television-watching. But to learn something new and combine it with another task is asking for trouble.

EFFECTIVE LEARNING TECHNIQUES

Now that we're aware of the commonly used less effective ways to learn, as well as the common misconceptions people tend to have about learning, it's a good time to delve into what some actual effective learning techniques are. The following are the techniques for learning that have the most solid basis in research, those which scientists are confident of in their ability to help with advancing your learning.

Only four such techniques are mentioned here. You may feel that a bigger list would be more helpful, but consider that these are the most helpful *proven* ways for better learning. Many of these techniques were also found as beneficial in John Dunlosky and his fellow researchers' review of 10 major learning techniques. Rather than being tempted to fall back into old habits, perhaps into some of the poor learning habits mentioned in the prior section as less effective, it will be more worth your while to invest effort into the following techniques. There are no promises for quick learning with no effort here. However, these are the techniques which will be most likely to get you results in your learning. The important part of course is to get into the habit of using them consistently.

Practice Testing

Practice testing is when you practice testing yourself over material that you wish to learn. It doesn't mean being tested in a formal environment where you will receive an evaluation that influences your future. Of course, through school we often think of tests as what teachers give us to test our knowledge over a section of the book, or lectures that the teacher has given. Many students will tend to build a negative perception of such tests. Since they often require study, which takes time and effort, testing tends to have a poor reputation among students. They would much rather do something else. Also, if a student doesn't study he may then find that he performs poorly and is also left with a bad feeling about testing.

Really, testing can be much broader than this. Practice testing can involve mental recall of the main points that you need to know. It can involve looking through keywords that you want to master, and covering up the definitions, testing yourself first before you look to the definitions. It doesn't have to be a painful experience, where you receive a letter grade, for example.

Testing yourself is one of the more useful techniques you can use to learn. This may be a bit surprising, because testing is usually thought of as an evaluation. When you're tested at school, you'll often get a letter grade and then you move on to the next lesson. But really, for testing to have a great effect in your learning, it should be used regularly. Someone who tests herself will have a much better understanding of any gaps in her knowledge. If she can't recall something important, she can look it up. Then she could test herself again later. By the time she takes a real test, or by the time she needs to apply the knowledge, she will be much more likely to remember it over someone who did not test herself.

This has been found to be a very effective technique. It's unfortunate that many students may naturally be put off by this learning technique. They're unlikely to realize how beneficial it can be, and they're likely to associate it with school tests that they are tired of dealing with. But an alternative way to view practice testing is just to see them as quizzes that are there to help keep you on the right track. It's easy to become overconfident and feel that you are making progress, but if you commit yourself to a regular quiz, perhaps weekly, you'll be much better able to gauge your progress and any weaknesses that need extra attention.

The way that you begin practice testing is to form questions based on what you are learning. If you are learning through school, you can possibly use questions already mentioned in your textbook or questions that your instructor has given you. If you are guiding your own learning, then you can ask questions on the level that you are trying to learn. If you are trying to learn on a very broad thematic level, then you can ask very broad questions. If reading a book, for example, you could form a question that gets at the big idea for each chapter. If you need more detail, you could ask a question for each section of the chapter. You have options as to how to test yourself, and you should keep in mind what you wish to learn and the kinds of questions that will aid your progress.

Distributed Practice

Distributed practice means splitting up study or learning sessions. Rather than cramming all the information that you need to know on the last day possible, it's much more beneficial to distribute practice or learning. You will learn more, understand more, and retain more if you split up your learning sessions.

The reason many students may continue to cram is because even though it's not the best way to learn, it does get some results. If someone hasn't done any studying, they will be better off cramming than not studying at all. However, they'd be much better off still by distributing their learning.

For example, if you want to learn U.S. History through a textbook with 15 chapters, it would make much more sense to read a chapter a week over 15 weeks, than to try to read the entire book in one day. It simply becomes too exhausting and doesn't give the brain enough time to work on building connections and a deep understanding of the material.

The distributed practice research applies more to learning in different domains, instead of learning specific skills like chess or bowling. For someone learning skills, there are other ideas to consider. For example, some physical skills may become exhausting after practicing them for too long. Also, some skills may require a mentor's time to help make sure that progress is being made.

With distributed practice, it's important to commit to this technique early on in your learning. If you find yourself behind on your learning and all of a sudden you need to catch up, it can become practically impossible to begin distributing your practice at that point. It may seem like a difficult commitment but it doesn't really have to be. What you will have to do is know your learning goal. What exactly are you trying to learn? Then split up that learning goal into roughly equal parts. If you want to learn how to cook 10 Italian recipes in the next few months, you could focus on cooking one new dish every week. At that rate it would take about 2 and a half months. As you may see, committing yourself to distributed practice is also a good way to make sure that you continue to make progress. It's easy to set a goal of wanting to learn something, but without steady progress it's also easy to fall behind. Then you may end up cramming, limiting your ability to learn well, or you may give up on the goal altogether. It's better to start using distributed practice from the beginning.

Interleaved Practice

Here is an interesting form of practice that may seem like a counterintuitive way to learn. With interleaved practice, as you learn, rather than stick to one rigid form of learning (e.g., just one concept, just one rule, or just one theme) you are much more open in the type of learning you engage in.

For example, if you are learning basketball, you may want to practice making free throw shots and to perfect that skill before you move on to other areas of your game. You'll be inclined to do this because it feels more focused. You are just doing free throws, and putting all of your energy into that, and so you'll make progress faster, right? Not necessarily. The research shows that you would be better off mixing up your practice. You might want to practice free throws for 15 minutes, then move on to practicing making passes, then move on to practicing blocking shots from other players.

The reason this can be a counterintuitive way to learn is that it may feel off or wrong at first. You may be practicing one part of a skill, or learning one subtopic within a larger topic, and feel that you need more time to fully grasp that one thing. It may feel like too much of a stretch to move on to other parts, but that's just what interleaved practice calls for.

In time, you will find yourself very confident in multiple skill sets if you consistently work toward making progress in different but related skill areas. The key part is to continue to struggle through in the beginning when it seems overwhelming.

Teaching and Explaining

Another good way to learn material is to teach it. First, it's important to learn the basics of an area. You may do this through reading or attending classes. When having amassed enough knowledge that the material is all in your mind, but you're not fully aware of what is important or how everything interconnects, it could be a good time to begin teaching or explaining the concepts to someone else. It is possible to engage in this without needing to teach someone else. You could just talk it through on your own, but there are more benefits in actually teaching the material to someone who isn't informed on the topic.

By teaching someone, you will be able to find any weaknesses in your understanding. Let's say you needed to learn an entire process, such as how to take and develop photographs, the old fashioned way, not digitally. As you explain the process, your naïve learner may ask all sorts of questions. Why do you have to bathe the photograph in chemicals? Why do you have to develop the photographs in the dark? By answering such questions (or attempting to), you will be more likely to make deeper connections and fully remember the process when you need to. Also, as with self-testing, you are likely to figure out any weaknesses in your knowledge by explaining it to someone else. If you find that a simple question stumps you, you will then realize that you need to study that particular section more carefully.

As mentioned in the myths of learning earlier in this book, it can be easy to feel overconfident that you know something when you actually don't. When you do find yourself feeling confident, or even if you don't, go ahead and explain the process or materials you are learning to someone else. If you are confident, you may find that there are still some areas of the material that you don't know as well as you should. If you aren't confident, you will also gain a better perspective of what you know and don't know.

One of the big benefits of teaching and explaining concepts to someone else is that they can ask any kind of question at all. You may get questions that you never would have expected, but that's fine. Do your best to answer any questions. Try to work through them logically and using everything you know. If you still can't determine the answer, simply look it up or ask a professor or expert if you know any.

WORK ON YOUR LEARNING TOOLKIT

First, what is your Learning Toolkit? It's just a set of tools that you have at your disposal to learn new things. Many of us acquire these throughout our lives naturally without thinking much about specific tools we can add to our arsenal to improve our learning. However, we do stand to gain from stopping to think about it. If you consider some of the ways of thinking and learning proposed in this section, you will be better for it. You'll find that your learning will become more efficient, enjoyable, and that you'll be better prepared to accomplish your learning goals.

Learn through Multiple Modes and Sources

Multimodal learning means *not* taking all of your learning in through one source. First of all, every source is biased in some way and prone to errors. When you learn through different sources, you'll become familiar with the biases that different sources have. In being aware of those biases, you'll be able to decide for yourself where you stand on any controversial issues, becoming aware of how all of the different sides feel about a topic. There also may be errors or other problems with any source you go to. There are often multiple ways to accomplish something, such as a skill. So it is possible that in one source you will learn a specific technique, but if you go to another source, they will teach a different technique. In the end, there are many perspectives, but there may be some actual errors, and you will never be aware of them unless you seek out learning from multiple sources.

Learning through multiple modes becomes more important the more that you want to attain expertise or mastery in a topic. If you really just need a broad overview or general feel of a topic, a Wikipedia page may be sufficient for your needs. But if you want to know a field inside and out, it's essential to seek out information from different sources.

What are some examples of learning through multiple modes? There are many, many ways. There are: teachers, mentors, school or college classes, free online courses, books and audiobooks, peers, online forums, podcasts, theater plays, hobby classes, etc. You can also learn through multiple sources even within one mode. For example, you could study mathematics by looking through two or three different textbooks. Perhaps you will find it helpful to work out different kinds of practice problems and seeing the same concepts explained in different ways in the textbooks.

Everyday life experiences could be one of your learning sources. You may go to a museum and talk to an expert attendant about dinosaurs. You may meet someone who tells you an extravagant story that inspires you to learn more. You may discuss the fermentation of wines while having a drink with a friend who happens to know a great deal about the topic. One of the great things about learning through various modes and sources is that you don't need to feel that you have to stick to one way of learning. If you absolutely dislike learning in a classroom format, you don't need to. You can read, find a mentor, or join a podcast.

Put Effort into your Learning

When you force yourself to read a chapter of a book, perhaps for school, or just for the feeling that you're accomplishing something, you may finish it realizing that you really have little idea of what the importance of the chapter was. On the other hand, when you find yourself completely absorbed by the material, making connections to how it relates to your past, and thinking up scenarios as to how you can use the information in the future, and the implications for other areas of your life, you'll find that you understand the material and its significance much better later on.

There are many ways we can put in more effort into our learning. We can challenge ourselves to think. Think about how what you're learning effects you. How does it affect other objects or people in your life? What would happen if you tried to apply what you're learning to someone else, or another time period, or a different location? Are there other concepts you've learned in the past that relate to what you're learning now in some way? Asking yourself questions is a good way to get yourself thinking, and to apply effort in your learning.

You can apply the same concept if you are learning a skill. Don't keep everything the same. Time yourself. Can you push yourself to go a bit faster? Can you perform the task more accurately? Can you spend more time practicing a particularly difficult part of the task? Can you somehow make the task more challenging? Perhaps even if you purposely make the task extremely difficult, there will still be something to learn. For example, an intermediate chess player, although highly unlikely to beat a Grandmaster (the highest chess title), could likely learn a great deal from playing such a game. He may learn advanced strategies and the Grandmaster may even give some pointers as to how the intermediate player could improve his game.

Of course, it isn't fun to lose. But we have to find a way to be comfortable with loss. To stay too much in our comfort zone, not challenging ourselves or pushing ourselves to put in more effort, will likely result in a mediocre accomplishment. The more we challenge ourselves, the more effort we will need to put in. The more effort we put in, the more likely we are to learn a great deal from our experiences.

We have to realize that learning isn't a task just like any other. You don't just schedule a block of time to learn, and then the learning happens, and you're done. It is a very active process that requires a good deal of effort in order to truly make the difference. You must focus on putting in the effort needed to meet your goal. Just be cautious not to get distracted with thinking too much about the result you want. Those results are more likely to come when you apply a consistent effort through time.

Review Already Learned Material

You may find that when you've learned something, you view it as permanently known and stored information. Unfortunately, memory does degrade over time, and for many of us we will begin to forget learned things. Even if you have a great memory, if you've learned a lot of material, such as if you've memorized 100 vocabulary words in prior weeks and successfully recalled them, you will find that as weeks pass it's easy to forget some of those words. Without reviewing what you've learned occasionally to refresh, you may forget it completely.

One way to get around the need to review, somewhat, is to actively use the information you are learning every day. But if you think about it, that in itself is a form of review.

If we allow months or years to pass, we will be less and less likely to recall material that was learned in the past. Imagine someone who goes to college and gets their bachelor's degree in mechanical engineering, but when they finish the program, rather than get a job in that field they get a job as a graphic designer. Ten years later, which skills and abilities will be more solid in the mind? Of course, many of the engineering principles will have faded from memory for lack of use, and many of the graphic design principles will be completely ingrained from the many years of learning and actively using that knowledge regularly.

Preview What is Coming up Ahead

You can think of this as either **pre-learning**, or as a **previewing** of what you will be learning coming up. This tool will be more important when you are dealing with new or challenging ideas. One good area to use this tool would be with learning mathematics.

It can help to have an idea of the concepts and ideas you will be learning before you actually learn them. Of course, pre-learning is a form of learning, but at this point you are just trying to get a rough overview. If you see some interesting concepts, you may go ahead and learn the definitions, but you are not trying to learn the material completely at this point yet.

The point of your pre-learning will be to gain an overall idea of the topic, to help you better absorb the material when you actively begin to learn it, or before you will be taught. If you find yourself getting lost in minute details of what you're learning, it may be a good idea to even seek resources outside of your main material. For example, if you normally use a specific math textbook, you may seek information from another resource that focuses on gaining a general understanding of big concepts. Perhaps you can find a resource or website that explains concepts graphically and through real world examples, rather than through just formulas.

If you are learning in a classroom, or through presentations, or any way in which you only have one chance to really absorb the material, it can be especially useful to do some pre-learning. Pre-learning will help prime and prepare you for the material that you really need to learn. If something is confusing, you're likely to notice this when you preview the material. Then you can figure out the cause of the confusion before your learning session begins. By the time the session begins, you'll be much more prepared and ready to understand the material.

Engage in Active Learning

This has been a theme of this book, but it's an important one. You have to have the want, the will, the curiosity, the drive to learn. It doesn't help to have the expectation that just the right material you need will land on your lap, and that just the right way to think about the material will be pre-digested for you and given to you, and that the answers will all be clearly explained just for you to understand. Even though these things just mentioned may seem ideal, as if you could take anything you wanted to learn and just absorb it through a television screen while having a snack, it's actually not how true learning works. Yes, occasionally you may come across a great documentary or a great learning resource through a television program. The point here isn't to diminish any one way of learning, it's that in order to fully comprehend a topic, we have to be prepared to work to figure it out. Hardly if ever is a learning resource designed specifically for us personally.

What is the difference between **active learning** and **passive learning**? An active learner will seek out new experiences in the world, whereas a passive one may engage in routine activities. An active learner will ask questions, whereas a passive one won't ask many questions, or will disregard them if he has any. An active learner, more importantly, will seek out answers to those questions. If one resource doesn't have them, he'll move on to the next. If he finds that he has a fundamental hole in his understanding of a domain, he may go back to more basic resources to try to understand the basics first. It's very possible that asking a few questions will lead to more and more questions, and the active learner may easily read multiple books or learn from multiple sources just to answer those questions. The passive learner may do an internet search or seek out information from one source, but he is unlikely to pursue answers to any follow up questions unless he is forced to.

We live in a world with such an abundance of learning opportunities. There is no reason to sit back passively and wait for someone to teach us something. We should seek out the teachers that can help further our learning. Some of these teachers may come in the form of books, videos, online sources, Wikipedia, friends, etc. There is no one formal teacher that you need to learn anything. You just need the will to learn and persistence.

Marilyn vos Savant has been recognized in the past by the Guinness Book of World Records as having the world's highest IQ. They no longer use this category, possibly because it is difficult to pin point one single person as the smartest individual in the world by using IQ scores. In any case, in an interview, she made some interesting comments about learning in an active way. She mentioned being aggressive intellectually, which I take to be a form of being active in learning. Here is what she said about how children often learn:

> *Children are sitting there and they are taught and told what to believe, they are passive from the very beginning, and one must be very aggressive intellectually to have a high IQ. The child is taught right from the beginning, which is a passive process. He or she sits there, and they simply try to believe everything they are told. For example, a five year old will believe anything we tell them. Right from the beginning people begin to believe what they are told - they begin to believe what they read in newspapers, hear on the radio, and see on television. They never learn to think independently.*

Her assessment seems accurate but somewhat grim. By allowing ourselves to passively take in information, to assume the information we take in is accurate rather than to investigate, can lead us to poor thinking, and to being led by whoever comes in to lead us. In order to think independently, we must start with learning more actively, being more aggressive in our efforts to understand.

She also shared something about her own upbringing, which gives us an idea as to how her parents may have influenced her own ability to become an active learner. She said:

> If I asked my mother a silly childish question, she would say "I'm not here to entertain you. You should go out and find the answer to that question." As a child everything is fascinating. If you learn how to go out and find the information, you can hardly be stopped later.

The important thing to realize here is that Marilyn vos Savant, one of the smartest recognized individuals in the world, was raised in a way where she was not given information, but encouraged to seek it out for herself. She acquired the habit of building up her curiosity and finding answers for herself, a manner of learning that is foreign even to many adults. This is a habit we should make efforts to change if we haven't already.

Pursue Graduated Challenges

In "The Art of Learning," Josh Waitzkin, a chess master, describes growing up playing chess. He mentioned that he had known of a boy who had not lost a chess game in over a year. Josh soon came to realize that all this boy did was play games against much weaker opponents. Often he played against complete beginners that didn't understand the game at all. The boy clearly had some skill, but he wasn't pushing himself to advance his learning by never challenging himself. In time, Josh pushed himself and played against tougher and tougher opponents, while the boy who never lost a game would refuse to play anyone with great skill. He continued to play very inexperienced players. Of course, Josh continued to improve his game, and the boy who never lost stagnated, not improving his game at all.

The principle to take away here is not to grow too comfortable as we learn. A part of learning is allowing ourselves to come into situations that make us uncomfortable and that push us further along in our abilities. They may even push us to the limits. This is a far better environment for learning than purposely choosing to avoid all challenges and always taking the easy way. In the end, those who have challenged themselves the most will make the greatest progress. Those who have been afraid to lose or make a mistake will stagnate, and have little progress to show for their time.

What is meant by graduated challenges is to become sensitive to the level of challenge you subject yourself to. If one level becomes too comfortable or easy, it's time to increase the challenge. We shouldn't become too comfortable in the sense of letting everything become too easy and staying at one level for too long. What we should learn to be comfortable with is the chance of loss or error. With great losses come the chance for great learning.

Be a Generalist and a Specialist

The more general information we have, the more we are able to build new connections. Remember that anytime you learn something new, you are building on a prior foundation. It can be quite practical to pursue a good general understanding of many topics and fields. This way, you will be more able to form new connections more easily. Also, when you do choose to specialize in something, you'll have many more connections to build off of.

A danger of specializing in one thing to the isolation or ignorance of all other fields is that you can miss obvious connections. You may miss a greater context and waste valuable time studying something that has already been answered within a different field. Also, by being aware of other topics and fields, you can use information from them to draw important analogies to your own field. Perhaps you will find that another system works similarly to a system you use every day.

There are different ways to be a generalist for your own purposes. A true generalist may study different topics and fields seemingly at random, seeking to learn just enough about most topics to have a general understanding. On the other hand, someone who sees themselves as more of a specialist may prefer to study fields outside to their own, but which are still somewhat overlapping. For example, a biologist may study chemistry and physics. A sociologist may study psychology and politics. Either strategy of being a generalist can be useful. Learning in a wide range of fields can be good to stimulate creativity and learning things by chance that may help or relate in other areas of your life. Learning in fields that are related to your primary interests can also help to make sure that you are able to learn more deeply about your true interest. You may come out with a much greater understanding of your topic than others who do not study those related topics.

It's also important to be a specialist because to some extent, in today's society we're all generalists. We are all bombarded by a wide range of information on a daily basis. There is radio, news, commercials and advertisements (which are a source of information too, even if biased), and so forth. With computers, the internet, smartphones and such devices, information travels fast and constantly. We can't keep up with it all. But if you make an effort to keep up with some of the new information, whether you use Twitter, Facebook, read news, go to online Forums, etc., you'll find that certain key pieces of information tend to float around. They may relate to big political events, celebrity news, funny videos, viral videos that appeal to emotion, a new nutritional finding, etc. Sooner or later you will find that some pieces of information float around more easily. To some extent this makes us general learners. Of course, it's good to take your learning into your own hands and decide what kind of topics you should pursue further. The kinds of outlets mentioned earlier often only discuss a topic on a surface level.

Immerse Yourself in the Topic

If you want to truly learn something, one of the best ways to advance your understanding and learn it fast (through real effort) is to completely immerse yourself in the topic. The military has been known to train its members in languages by sending them to a country that speaks the desired language and having them learn by living in that environment. In order to survive and get by, the soldiers must quickly learn at least the basics of the language. Often, they're able to quite rapidly learn to communicate, even if the grammar is imperfect.

A level of immersion that intense, where you completely change your way of life in order to learn a concept, won't be realistic for most people. It can be a great way to learn, that's for sure, but due to the impracticality of it, I would suggest trying a more manageable type of immersion, where travel could be voluntary but not necessary.

With this less intense version of immersion, when learning a language (or anything else) you could do any of a variety of activities to try to create an environment of language learning. Let's say the language were Spanish. You could put up Latin American country maps around your home. You could put up ornaments or paintings or other sorts of decorations around your home that are of Latin American or Spanish origin. You could invite an international student to stay in your home and learn some Spanish from her. It makes sense, of course, to take some sort of a beginner course in Spanish to begin learning the vocabulary and grammar, but in the spirit of immersion the learning should go further than that. Remember, in true immersion you would be completely surrounded by Spanish speakers (or whatever language you would choose), by the culture, and there would be no way to give up and quit. You should of course practice that same level of persistence. Challenge yourself and don't give up so easily. Keep a Spanish to English dictionary on you, or an app that does so, so you can quickly learn words as they come up. As you continue to learn, you could search for a friend on Skype who speaks Spanish natively. You could have conversations with the person. Also, you could begin reading forums online in Spanish, and participating in the discussion. You may find local groups that practice or that support Spanish or Latin American culture in some way. Also, you could go to a Spanish speaking restaurant and practice ordering a meal in Spanish. You see, there are so many ways to practice a level of immersion in your own way, without absolutely needing to travel. The way the world is setup now, we can experience other parts of the world virtually using the internet.

The point of immersion is that as you surround yourself by one topic, you prepare yourself to learn it completely. In a matter of a month or two it's possible to make as much progress as someone else might make in years of study. Of course, in order to make that kind of progress it would take a complete commitment to the goal of learning a language, or whatever the goal may be. It does not need to be language. You could take a similar approach if you wanted to learn music or any other skill.

CONCLUSION:

WHAT TYPE OF LEARNER WILL YOU BE?

You should have a good background in the learning process and what you can do to improve your learning at this point. Now, where do you go from here? How will you apply the learning principles of this book in your life? Of course, we all learn naturally every day, but to really make progress we must have goals and work purposefully to accomplish them. If we just rely on learning as being something that happens to us, we will be very passive and therefore not make much progress.

The truth is there isn't one quick formula to help you be a master learner, or to master any one topic. There is no true shortcut in the sense that you can just apply one technique or strategy for learning and you will therefore achieve mastery in that area with little study or effort.

What there is, however, are proven techniques and approaches to learning that can help you achieve your goals. Also, through practicing your learning, you can become a better learner. At first, you may need to look back at this book or others to make sure you stay on track in progressing with your learning. You may try to follow the learning process laid out, at least roughly. That could be a good way to start. As time passes you will internalize the learning process and everything you can do to improve your learning. You may find yourself on your way to building up skill in one or several domains. With enough practice, you could even master the skill of learning.

First, it's important to choose an approach to learning. It might have made sense to cover this section much earlier in the book, but now that you are almost ready to begin learning, or to advance your learning, I believe it makes even more sense to discuss here. There are three overall approaches to learning that you can take, going into the future. This is mainly directed to independent learners, which I would encourage you to be. Even if you take part in a structured curriculum through school, you can always benefit from continuing to learn on your own. I'd encourage you to use one of the following approaches to learning. You could even combine them if you'd prefer.

The Exploratory Generalist

The exploratory generalist will always be seeking out new forms of information. He isn't so interested in mastering any one particular topic, rather he wants to learn as much as he can about a variety of fields. He will likely have an immense curiosity, always interested in discovering new things.

This approach will be great for someone who is endlessly curious, or someone who is young and hasn't yet discovered their life mission. This approach will also often favor a creative mind. A creative person will want exposure to as many kinds of information as they can get, in order to draw from a great variety of ideas to help stimulate their creativity. Also, someone who simply prefers to be informed on a wide range of topics, who perhaps enjoys being able to help people with all kinds of problems, will be well suited to this learning approach.

The exploratory generalist may enjoy going to the library and reading a chapter from one book, then reading a chapter from another book, and so forth. He may like reading a new Wikipedia page every day. He might like visiting new Museums, watching documentaries, Ted Talks, and engaging in lively discussions about all sorts of topics.

Obviously, the exploratory generalist isn't so caught up in following a specific structured curriculum. Every day is viewed as a new learning opportunity, and this kind of learner may have very general objectives, such as to learn more about medieval history or to understand quantum physics better. Really, the topic could be anything, but rather than specialize in the topic, the exploratory generalist is interested in acquiring a general understanding of the topic. If a particular topic is especially interesting, there is nothing stopping him from delving deeper into the topic through further research.

The Project Tackler

The project tackler (someone who tackles projects) wants some level of structure to her learning. Yet, she doesn't want such a high level of structure that everything is all planned out. She wants freedom to switch domains or to change direction as she likes, but still she wants some level of commitment so that she can actually make progress in her learning. The project tackler may be concerned that if she doesn't pick specific projects to finish, then nothing will ever get done. The exploratory way of learning may have too much freedom and make her uncomfortable.

A project tackler will be someone who tends to be practical. She will not want to begin learning something unless she feels some specific learning outcome will come out of it. She'll probably have a preference for size of her projects. If she tends to get bored after doing something for a month, she may specifically choose projects that can be finished within that time period. If she feels the need to accomplish something every week then she may choose very small projects that can be completed in that time frame.

You may want an example of a project at this point. It's just as it sounds. The project doesn't need to be formal in anyway, although it can be. But they can be completely defined by the project tackler. An example would be if someone decided that they wanted to learn 1,000 words of Italian using the online program Memrise, which is like a flash card program. The project tackler could set time goals, or leave them open. The point is that she has a concrete project that she wishes to finish. Another example would be that the project is to learn how to play one song on piano. If the learner were a complete beginner at piano, then the project may be to work through the first 10 pages of a beginning piano book and play those songs with almost no mistakes. Again, there are no strict rules. The project tackler decides how she wishes to define her projects, whether they'll be shorter or longer, easier or more challenging. She can set time limits or leave them open ended.

The Curriculum Developer

The curriculum developer will not be fully satisfied with either of the prior learning approaches. He will want something much more structured and directed. He will want a clearly defined path that he can follow to meet his specific goals. Even though the curriculum developer wants structure, there is still much room for flexibility with this type of learning. You can choose to design a curriculum that centers all around one domain, or you can make a curriculum that involves learning about a great range of topics. Also, the curriculum can be designed to cover a month, a year, or any time span.

Someone who would like this approach to learning is likely to prefer to have control over their learning. They have specific skills, abilities, or knowledge they're interested in, and they don't want to be sidetracked by material that falls outside of that range. However the person who prefers this style isn't necessarily someone who always needs full control. It is possible that this person simply feels there is a great deal to learn, and he is so certain about what he wants to accomplish that he wants to create a path that will get him to his goals in the fastest way possible. It's possible that this style of learner has used the exploratory generalist approach or the project tackler approach in the past, but now that he knows his path, he prefers to take a much more structured approach.

You may realize that if you go through the university level of education, many professors will have a syllabus, which is a similar idea to the curriculum developer approach to learning. However, the point here is that it's not always possible or desired to go through formal schooling. Perhaps you know enough in your domain already that you feel confident outlining the key areas you need to learn and pursue in order to advance in your goals. In that case, going the independent route of creating your own curriculum could be a great option.

With this approach to learning, it can certainly help to have access to experts, but it's not always necessary. As part of the curriculum that you develop, you may include free online university courses (such as MOOCs), books to read, to approach experts or professors for an interview, locations to visit, etc. Anything that fits into the exact topics you want to learn can fit into the curriculum. It's possible that you want to learn a bit about everything, and you can still choose this style of learning over the exploratory generalist style. You may do your research and find 15 books or sources of information that you want to digest within a year in order to learn a bit about everything.

It can be a useful analogy to see yourself as the professor of your own course, and that you are designing the syllabus for that course. It's possible to include all kinds of sources in your class materials. You don't need to limit yourself just to books, videos, or practical experience. You can include all of these and more if you'd like.

Take Action

The whole point of this part of the book has really been just to serve as a reminder that you must take action in order to make progress on your learning. I would encourage you to choose one of the above three approaches to learning, but if you prefer a different way that is fine as long as you are taking action. I think it's a great step to want to improve your learning and having read through this book. I wish you the best on your learning goals and I hope you make great progress.

THANK YOU

Thank you for taking the time to read *No One Ever Taught Me How to Learn.* I hope that you found the information useful. Just remember that a key part of the learning process is putting what you read into practice.

Before you go, I want to invite you to pick up your free copy of *Step Up Your Learning: Free Tools to Learn Almost Anything.* All you have to do is type this link into your browser:

http://bit.ly/Robledo

Also, if you have any questions, comments, or feedback about this book, you can send me a message and I'll get back to you as soon as possible. Please put the title of the book you are commenting on in the subject line. My email address is:

ic.robledo@mentalmax.net

DID YOU LEARN SOMETHING NEW?

If you found value in this book, please review it on Amazon so I can stay focused on writing more great books. Even a short one or two sentences would be helpful.

To go directly to the review page, you may type this into your web browser:

http://hyperurl.co/oqmvg0

AN INVITATION TO THE "MASTER YOUR MIND" COMMUNITY (ON FACEBOOK)

I founded a community where we can share advice or tips on our journey to mastering the mind. Whether you want to be a better learner, improve your creativity, get focused, or work on other such goals, this will be a place to find helpful information and a supportive network. I hope you join us and commit to taking your mind to a higher level.

To go directly to the page to join the community, you may type this into your web browser:

http://hyperurl.co/xvbpfc

MORE BOOKS BY I. C. ROBLEDO

The Secret Principles of Genius

The Intellectual Toolkit of Geniuses

The Smart Habit Guide

55 Smart Apps to Level Up Your Brain

Ready, Set, Change

Idea Hacks

To see the full list of authored books, visit:

www.Amazon.com/author/icrobledo

Made in the USA
Middletown, DE
14 September 2020